REAL
NORWEGIANS
EAT
LUTEFISK
Rose Marie
Meuwissen
SAE

ISBN 10: 1-59298-294-8
ISBN 13: 978-1-59298-294-3

Library of Congress Catalog Number: 2009929121
Printed in the United States of America
First Printing: 2009
13 12 11 10 09 5 4 3 2 1

Beaver's Pond Press, Inc.
7104 Ohms Lane, Suite 101
Edina, MN 55439-2129
(952) 829-8818
www.BeaversPondPress.com

www.realnorwegianseatlutefisk.com

To my father, Sverre Waagen.
Thanks for having the courage to come to a strange new land, America, over sixty years ago, and for keeping your Norwegian heritage and traditions alive for your children, grandchildren, and great-grandchildren.
-RM

To my grandfather, Alfred Engelstad.
Thanks for continually finding distant relatives and making them less distant.
-KF

RECIPE FOR LUTEFISK

4 lbs Lutefisk
1 lb Melted Butter

Skin lutefisk, rinse thoroughly in cold water.
Cut fish into serving size pieces.
Fill pan with cold salted water.
Place lutefisk in water and bring to a boil.
Simmer 3-10 minutes or until tender and translucent in color.

Serve with melted butter or white gravy.
Serves 8.

LUTEFISK
Codfish dried, then soaked two days in a
strong lye solution;
Then one day in fresh water.
SAE

Father cooks the Lutefisk.
He says it really is fish.
But it doesn't look like fish.
It looks like jello—
White, wiggly, jiggly jello.

Far koker Lutefisk.
Han sa det er virkelig fisk.
Men, det ser ikkje ut som fisk.
Det ser ut som gele`—
Kvit, vrikker, vipper gele`.

But it smells like fish.
The kitchen smells like fish.
My clothes smell like fish.
How can it look like jello?
White, wiggly, jiggly jello.

Men det lukta som fisk.
Kjøkkenet lukta som fisk.
Klærne mine lukta som fisk.
Korleis kan det sjå ut som gele`?
Kvit, vrikker, vipper gele`.

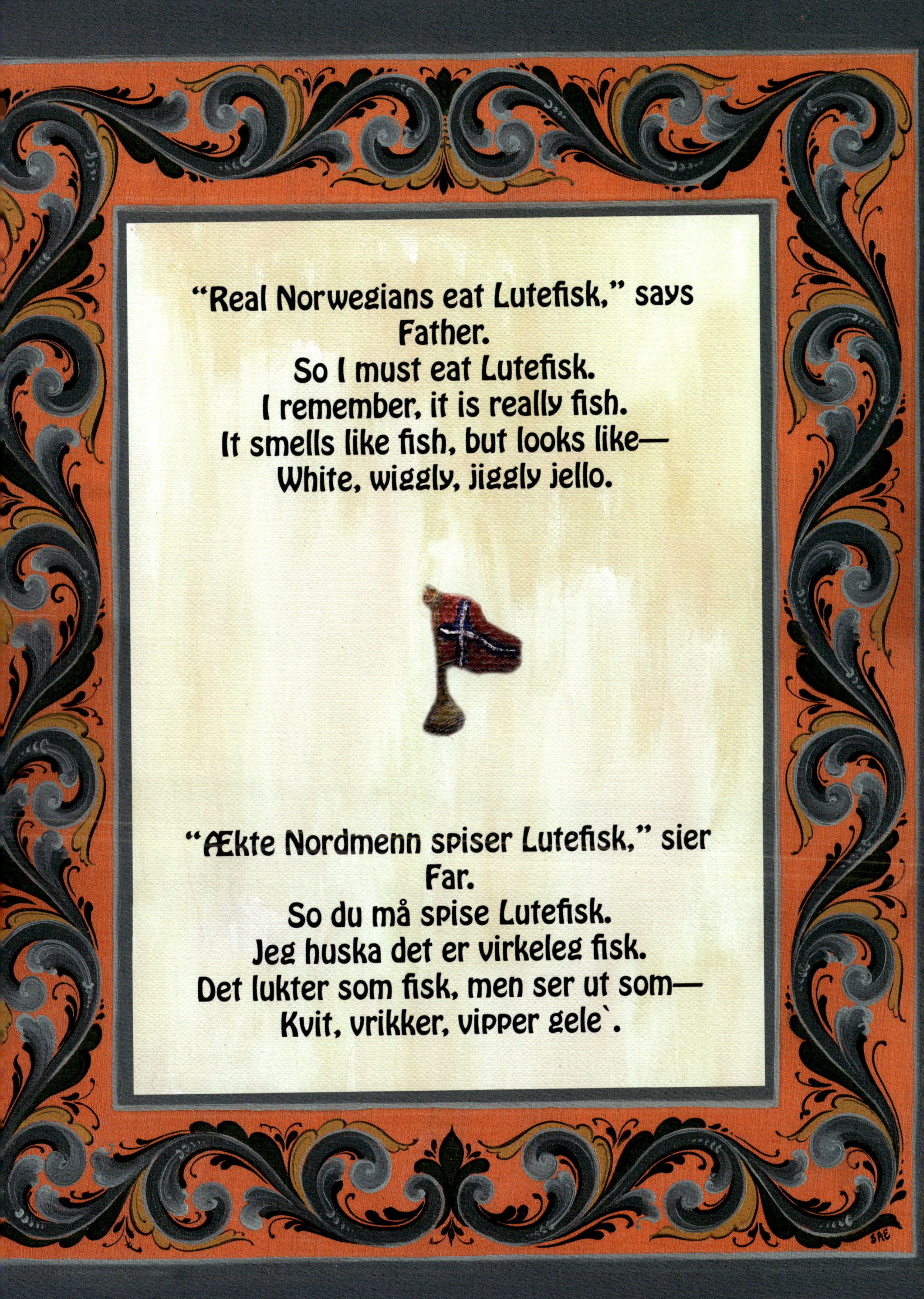
"Real Norwegians eat Lutefisk," says Father.
So I must eat Lutefisk.
I remember, it is really fish.
It smells like fish, but looks like—
White, wiggly, jiggly jello.
"Ækte Nordmenn spiser Lutefisk," sier Far.
So du må spise Lutefisk.
Jeg huska det er virkeleg fisk.
Det lukter som fisk, men ser ut som—
Kvit, vrikker, vipper gele`.
SAE

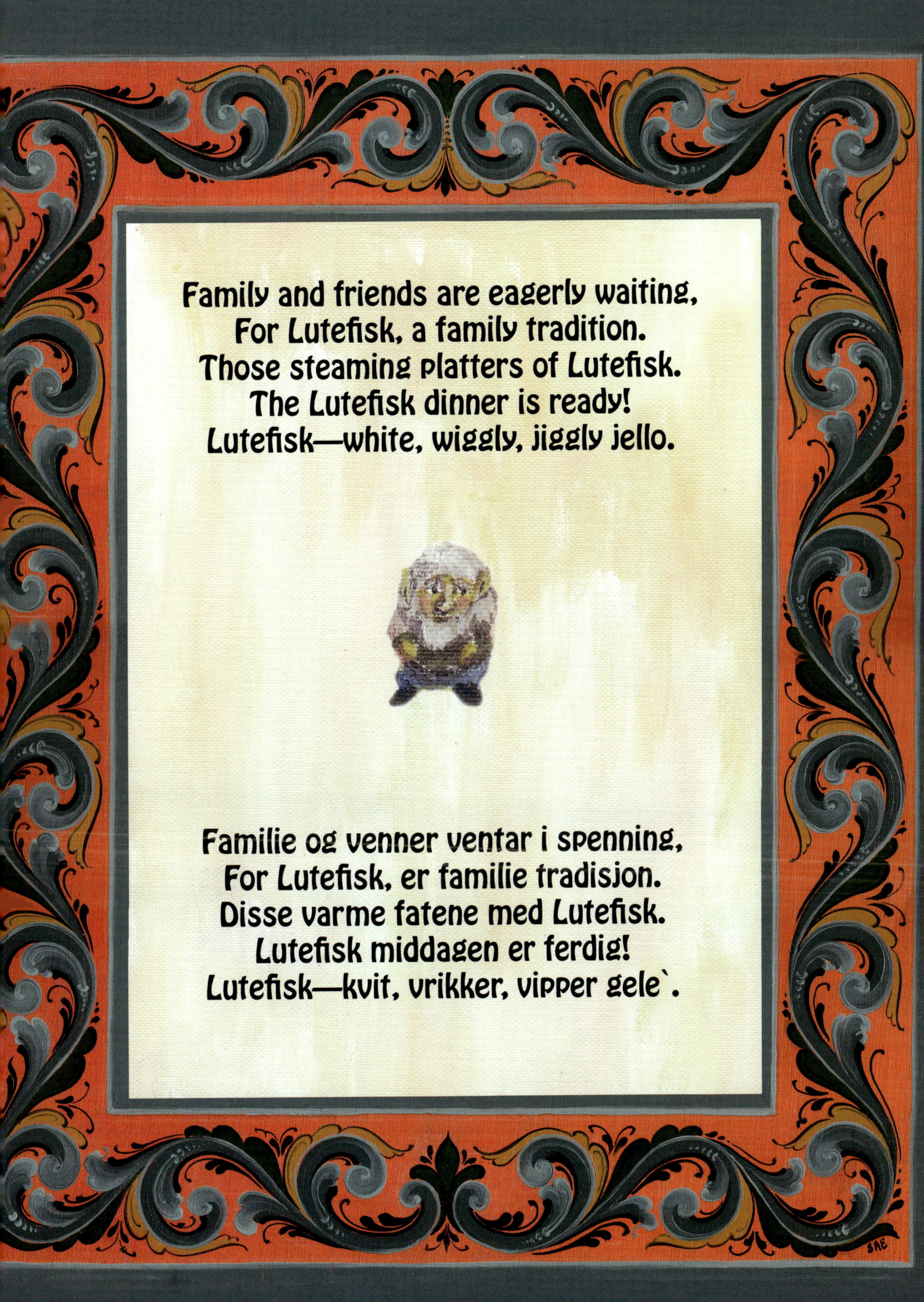

Family and friends are eagerly waiting,
For Lutefisk, a family tradition.
Those steaming platters of Lutefisk.
The Lutefisk dinner is ready!
Lutefisk—white, wiggly, jiggly jello.

Familie og venner ventar i spenning,
For Lutefisk, er familie tradisjon.
Disse varme fatene med Lutefisk.
Lutefisk middagen er ferdig!
Lutefisk—kvit, vrikker, vipper gele`.

"Real Norwegians eat Lutefisk," says
Father.
"You will like Lutefisk,
Smothered in melted butter or white gravy.
You will love Lutefisk.
Real Norwegians love Lutefisk."
"Ækte Nordmenn spiser Lutefisk," sier
Far.
"Du vil like Lutefisk,
Mye smelta smør eller kvit saus.
Du vil elske Lutefisk.
Ækte Nordmenn elsker Lutefisk."

I will close my eyes.
Maybe it tastes like fish.
But you cannot fool the mouth.
It says not fish; but jello—
White, wiggly, jiggly jello.
Jeg vil lukke øynene.
Kanskje det smaker som fisk.
Men du kan ikkje lure munnen din.
Den sier ikkje fisk, men gele`—
Kvit, vrikker, vipper gele`.
SAE

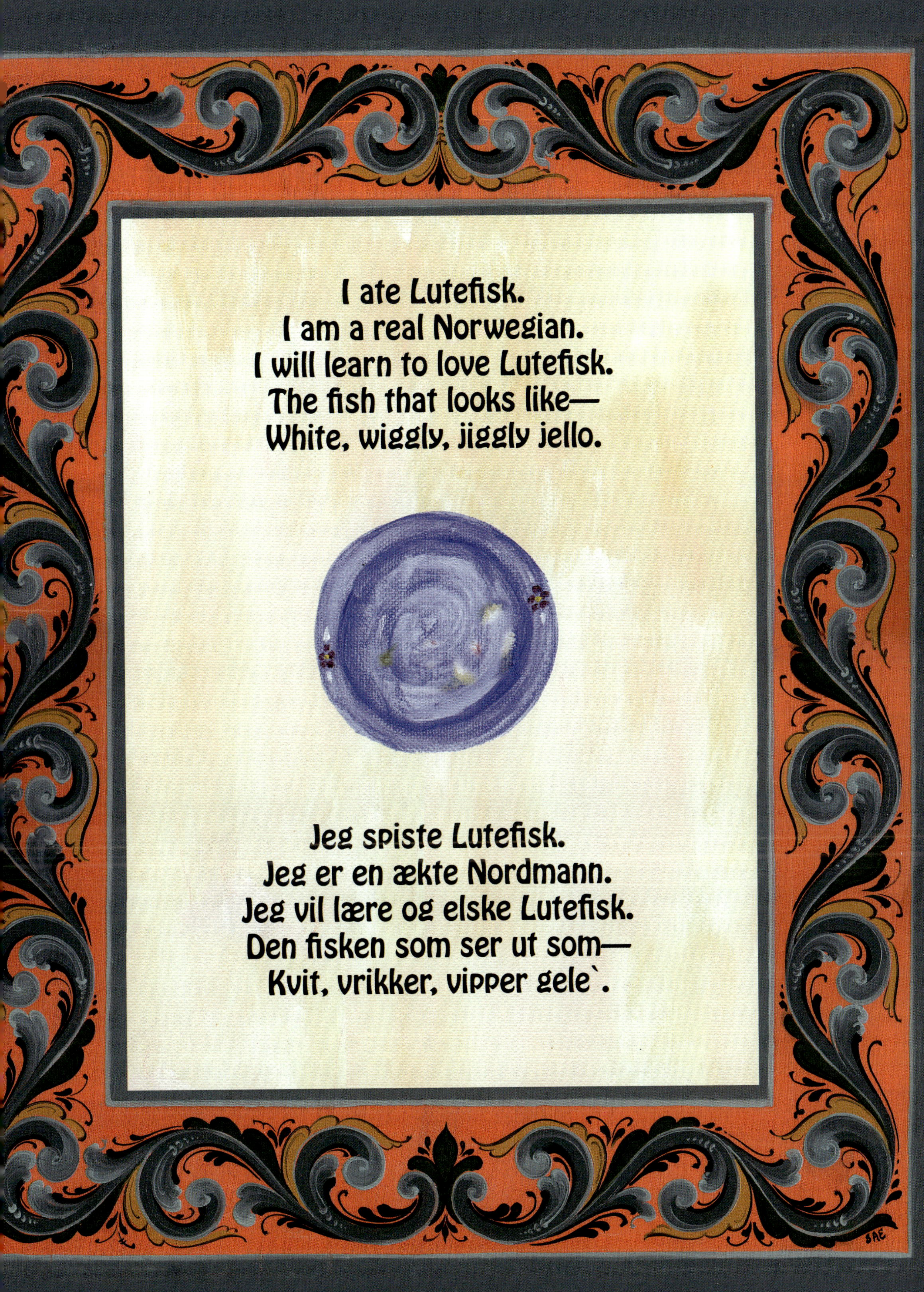
I ate Lutefisk.
I am a real Norwegian.
I will learn to love Lutefisk.
The fish that looks like—
White, wiggly, jiggly jello.
Jeg spiste Lutefisk.
Jeg er en ækte Nordmann.
Jeg vil lære og elske Lutefisk.
Den fisken som ser ut som—
Kvit, vrikker, vipper gele`.

I love jello.
I will love Lutefisk.
I can love Lutefisk.
I do love Lutefisk.
Lutefisk—white, wiggly, jiggly jello.

Jeg elsker jello.
Jeg vil elske Lutefisk.
Jeg kan elske Lutefisk.
Jeg elsker Lutefisk.
Lutefisk— kvit, vrikker, vipper gele`.

FAMILY TRADITIONS:
A family's way of celebrating special occasions which are handed down from one generation to the next.
FAMILINS TRADISJONER:
En families måte å feire spesielle anledninger på som er hentet fra en generasjon til den neste.

NORWEGIAN:
A native of Norway or a descendant of a native of Norway.
NORDMANN:
En innfødt fra Norge eller en etterkommer av en innfødt fra Norge.

FATHER:
The head of the family; a man who sires a child.
FAR:
En mann som har fått barn er en far.

FISH:
Cold blooded water creatures with fins and gills;
Some used for food.
FISK:
Kald blodet vannkreaturer med finner og gjeller; brukes som mat.

JELLO:
A gelatin like substance with a smooth glossy surface;
May be translucent in color or colored.
GELE`:
En gelatin med substans som en glatt skinnende overflate; kan være gjennomskinnelig eller farget.
SAE

LOVE:
To have strong feelings for someone or something.
KJÆRLIGHET:
Å ha sterke følelser for noen eller noe.

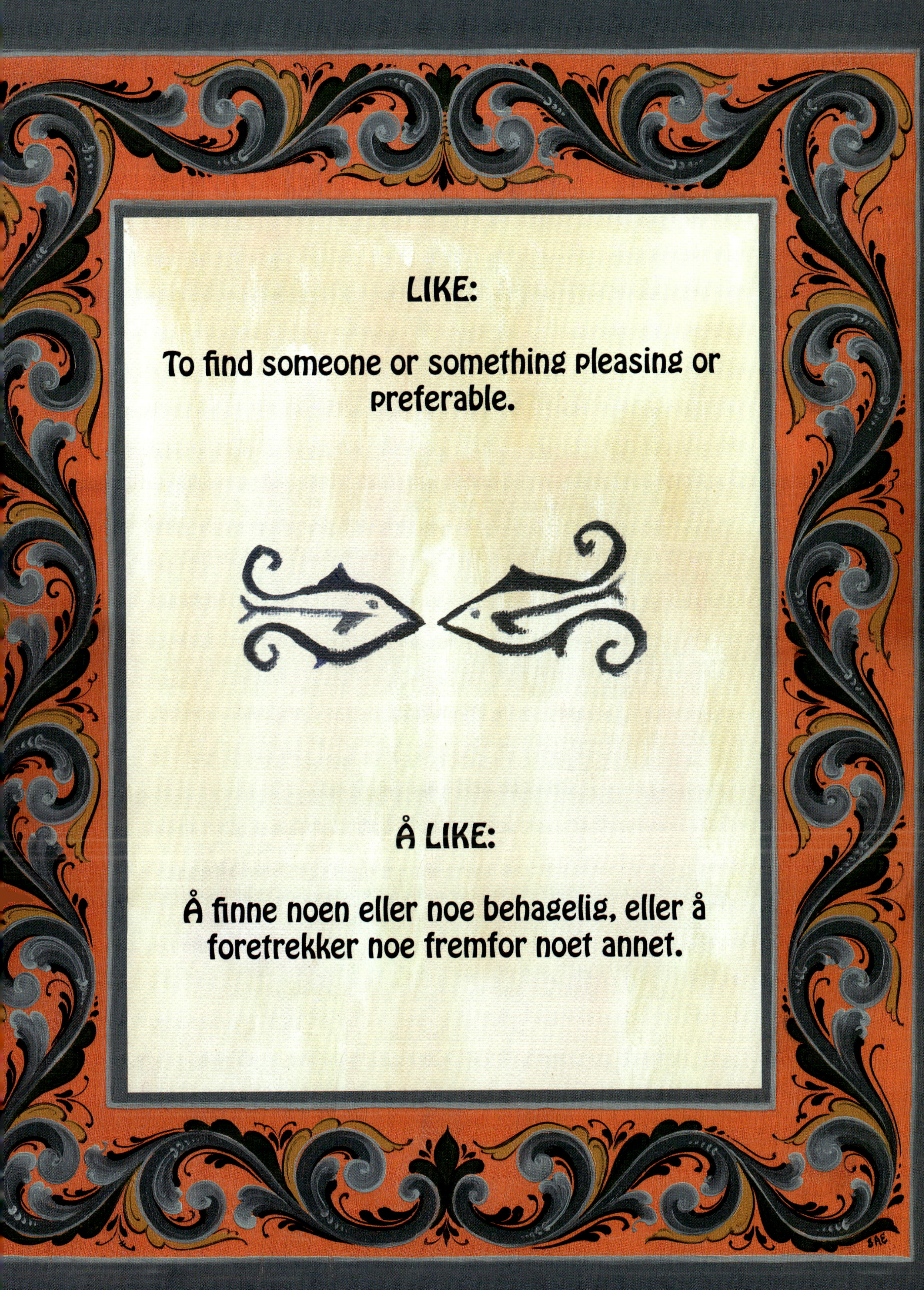
LIKE:
To find someone or something pleasing or preferable.
Å LIKE:
Å finne noen eller noe behagelig, eller å foretrekker noe fremfor noet annet.
BAE

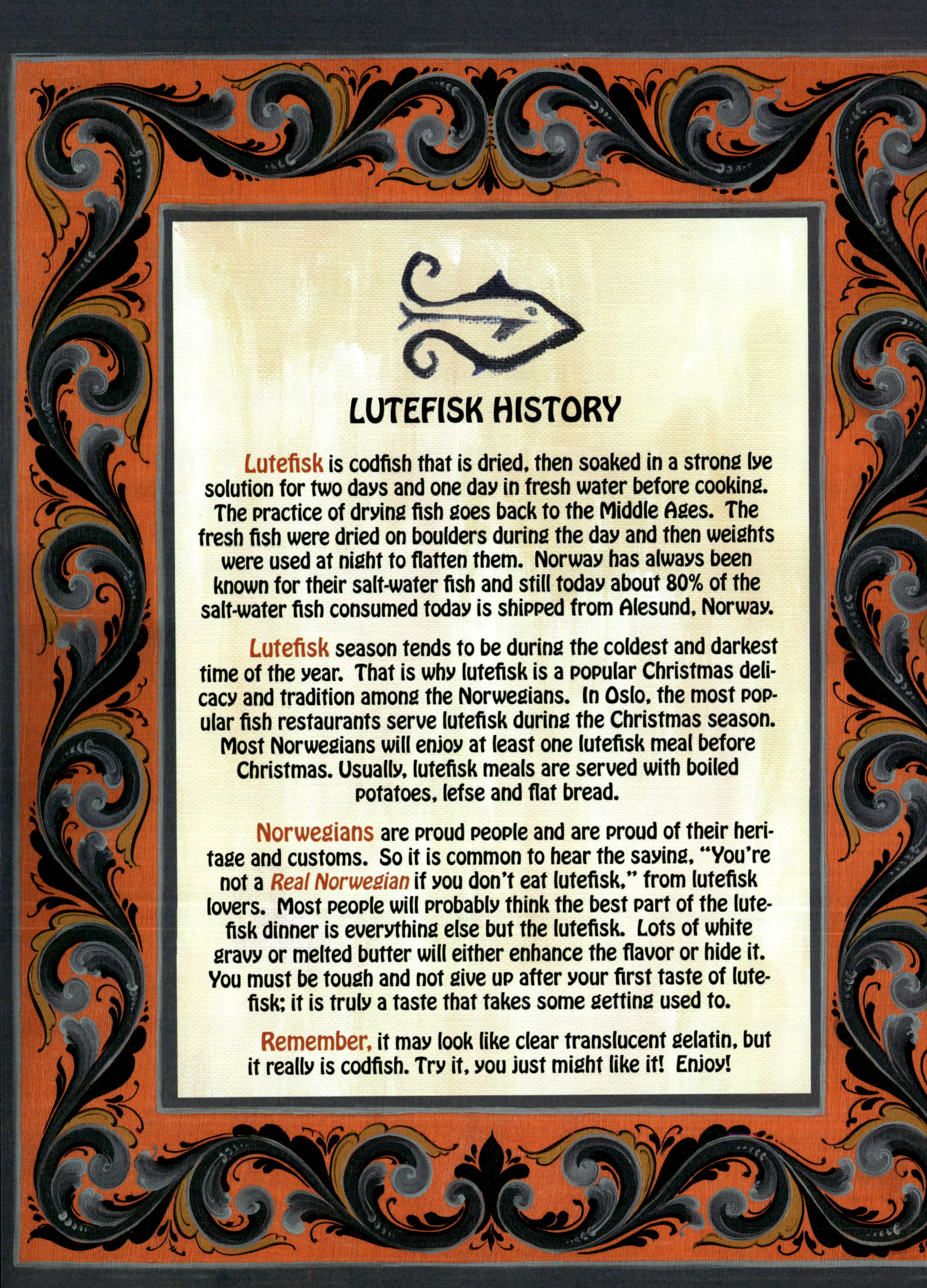

LUTEFISK HISTORY

Lutefisk is codfish that is dried, then soaked in a strong lye solution for two days and one day in fresh water before cooking. The practice of drying fish goes back to the Middle Ages. The fresh fish were dried on boulders during the day and then weights were used at night to flatten them. Norway has always been known for their salt-water fish and still today about 80% of the salt-water fish consumed today is shipped from Alesund, Norway.

Lutefisk season tends to be during the coldest and darkest time of the year. That is why lutefisk is a popular Christmas delicacy and tradition among the Norwegians. In Oslo, the most popular fish restaurants serve lutefisk during the Christmas season. Most Norwegians will enjoy at least one lutefisk meal before Christmas. Usually, lutefisk meals are served with boiled potatoes, lefse and flat bread.

Norwegians are proud people and are proud of their heritage and customs. So it is common to hear the saying, "You're not a *Real Norwegian* if you don't eat lutefisk," from lutefisk lovers. Most people will probably think the best part of the lutefisk dinner is everything else but the lutefisk. Lots of white gravy or melted butter will either enhance the flavor or hide it. You must be tough and not give up after your first taste of lutefisk; it is truly a taste that takes some getting used to.

Remember, it may look like clear translucent gelatin, but it really is codfish. Try it, you just might like it! Enjoy!

LUTEFISK HISTORIE

Lutefisk er codfisk som er tørket, da det gjennombløter i en sterk lye løsning for to dager og så tages i ferskvann før koking. Praksisen av å tørke fisk drar tilbake til Middle Alderen. Den ferske fisk tørket på berg eller steiner i løpet av dagen og då bruke vekter om natten til å flate dem ut. Norge var alltid kjent for deres salt vann fisk og enda i dag om 80% av saltet fisk som transporterer i dag er fra Ålesund, Norge.

Lutefisk sesong er tilbøyelig til være i løpet av det kaldeste og den mørkeste tid av året. Det er derfor lutefisk er en populær Jule finhet og tradisjon blant Nordmenn. I Oslo, den mest populære fisk restauranter serverer lutefisk i løpet av Jule sesong. Den meste Nordmenn spiser minst en lutefisk måltid før Jule. Vanligvis serveres lutefisk måltider med kokte poteter, lefse og flatt brød.

Nordmenn er stolt folk og er stolt av deres arv og toll. Så det er felles hørt ordspråk, "Du er ikke en *Virkelig Nordmann* om de ikke spiser Lutefisk," fra lutefisk elskere. Det meste folk tror sannsynlig vis den beste delen av lutefisk middag er alt annet en lutefisk. Min kvit saus or meltet smør vill enten effektivisere smaken eller gjemmer den. Ver tøff og ikke gir opp etter deres først smak av lutefisk; det er sant en smak som tar noen tid å venne seg til.

Husk, det ser ut som klar gjennomskinnelig gele, men det er virkelig codfisk. Prøv det, det er akkurat som det er noe! Nytt!

SAE

Rose Marie Meuwissen, author, has a Masters in Creative Writing from Hamline University. She is a first generation Norwegian-American and lives in Minneapolis, Minnesota. Her father, Sverre Waagen was born and raised in Norway and when he came to America after WWII, he brought along his Norwegian heritage and traditions to share with his family. Rose Marie has traveled often to Norway with her family and children to see their heritage and family history on the family farm located on a fjord in Gurskebotn, on the west coast of Norway. Her company, Nordic Treats, serves traditional Norwegian foods for Norway Day each year. Rose Marie wrote this book for both children and adults to promote the Norwegian language, traditions and, of course, Lutefisk. Heritage and traditions play an important part in children's lives by allowing them to find out where their ancestors came from and to learn about their family history which builds self-esteem and self-worth.
www.realnorwegianseatlutefisk.com

Kelly Frankenberg, illustrator, has a BFA in illustration from the Minneapolis College of Art & Design. She is originally from Minnesota and proud to be half Norwegian. Teaching and traveling give Kelly inspiration for her artwork. One of her favorite places to visit is Norway. She wishes to thank relatives, Ingrid Arntzen and Kari Standnes, for their Norwegian input with the book. Kelly's artwork can be seen in books, magazines, TV, film, and on her website.
www. Kellyfrankenberg.com

Shirley Evenstad, rosemaler, has a BS in Business Education from the University of North Dakota, studied with master Norwegian Rosemaling teachers at Vesterheim, the Norwegian American Museum in Decorah, Iowa and earned a Gold Medal in rosemaling from Vesterheim. She participated in painting the Norway Pavillion at the Epcot Center in Orlando, Florida. She is a native Minnesotan and resides in Minneapolis, Minnesota. Shirley has been rosemaling for over thirty years. She teaches rosemaling classes in Richfield, travels out of state to teach, and paints by commission.